FIRST
BIOGRAPHIES

# Rosa Parks

Published by Raintree Steck-Vaughn Publishers, an imprint of Steck-Vaughn Company

Planned and produced by The Creative Publishing Company
Editors: Christine Lawrie and Pam Wells

**Library of Congress Cataloging-in-Publication Data**

Holland, Gini.
    Rosa Parks / Gini Holland; illustrated by David Price.
       p.    cm. — (First biographies)
    Summary: A brief biography of the African American who, in refusing to obey a discriminatory rule about bus seating, set off both the Montgomery Bus Boycott and a movement that changed the nation's laws.
    ISBN 0-8172-4451-4
    1. Parks, Rosa, 1913- — Juvenile literature.    2. Afro-Americans — Alabama — Montgomery — Biography — Juvenile literature.    3. Civil rights workers — Alabama — Montgomery — Biography — Juvenile literature.    4. Afro Americans — Civil rights — Alabama — Montgomery — Juvenile literature.    5. Segregation in transportation — Alabama — Montgomery — History — 20th century — Juvenile literature.    6. Montgomery (Ala.) — Race relations — Juvenile literature.    7. Montgomery (Ala.) — Biography — Juvenile literature.
[1. Parks, Rosa, 1913-.    2. Civil rights workers.    3. Afro Americans — Biography.    4. Women — Biography.]    I. Price, David (David Charles), 1965-  ill.    II. Title.    III. Series.
F334.M753P3847    1997
323'.092 — dc20                    96-23015
[B]                                   CIP
                                        AC

Printed and bound in the United States
1 2 3 4 5 6 7 8 9 0 W 99 98 97 96

# FIRST BIOGRAPHIES

# Rosa Parks

Gini Holland
Illustrated by David Price

RSVP

RAINTREE
STECK-VAUGHN
PUBLISHERS
The Steck-Vaughn Company

*Austin, Texas*

Some people call Rosa Parks the mother of the civil rights movement, or cause. This is because she said a small word that made a big difference. She would not give up her seat to a white man just because he was white. When she said no to him, she helped change unfair laws that held African Americans down. These were called "Jim Crow" laws.

THIS PART OF THE BUS
FOR THE COLORED RACE

When Rosa was growing up, African Americans paid the same ten-cent bus fare as whites paid. But, in many southern towns, Jim Crow laws said that African Americans had to sit in the back of the bus. This was known as the "colored" part of the bus. These laws also said that if the "whites only" section was full, African Americans had to give their seats to white riders.

Rosa Parks was the first one to say no. She said it in a way that gave others in the South the courage to say no, too.

Rosa Parks was born in Tuskegee, Alabama, on February 4, 1913. Her mother's family knew all about the way of life that Jim Crow laws tried to keep going. Rosa's great-grandmother had been a slave. Her grandmother was five years old when slavery ended.

When Rosa was a toddler, her father went up North to look for work. At that time, it was hard for African-American men to get jobs, especially in the South. Rosa's mother went to live with Rosa's grandparents at a place called Pine Level. They owned twelve acres of land there. They had bought it from their slave owners after the family was set free.

Rosa's father came back to Pine Level for a while, then left again to find work. He visited when Rosa was five years old. Rosa did not see him again until she was grown up and married.

Rosa's mother was a teacher in Spring Hill. It was too far to walk to each day. So she stayed there all week and just saw her family on weekends. Rosa went to a "black school" with about fifty other students in a one-room schoolhouse in Pine Level.

In those days, Jim Crow laws said African-American children could not go to school with white children. White children went to school in buildings heated and paid for by taxes from both whites and blacks. Black families had to supply wood for heat and the money to run their schools with no help from taxes.

White students went to school for nine months each year. But African-American children could only go for five months because they were needed to help plant, chop, and pick cotton.

Rosa picked cotton from the age of six. It was hot, hard work. The boss, Mr. Freeman, called his workers bad names. But Rosa and her family needed the money, so they kept on picking.

It was good that Rosa's family raised chickens and cows, and had a garden. They fed themselves well. They sold eggs and calves to get other things they needed. Rosa's mother sewed all their clothes.

Not all white people in Pine Level were mean. Rosa remembers an "old, old white lady" who used to take her fishing. The old lady also visited her grandparents a lot.

From age eight to eleven, Rosa was taught by her mother in Spring Hill, but that school only went through sixth grade. Then, in 1924, she entered Miss Alice White's School. It was the first time she had been taught by a white teacher. Rosa had to live in Montgomery with relatives while she went to this school.

In Montgomery they had separate drinking
fountains for whites and "coloreds." Rosa used to
wonder if the "white" water tasted different from
"colored" water. But it was the same water. Black
people were not allowed to eat in the same
restaurants as white people. They also did not
have the same rights on buses.

During Rosa's childhood, the Ku Klux Klan often rode through the black community. The Klan was a secret group. They burned churches, and beat up and killed African Americans. The Klan also punished whites who treated African Americans fairly.

The Klan burned Miss White's school down twice before Rosa went there. They hated Miss White because segregation was supposed to keep white teachers for white children and "colored" teachers for "colored" children. The Klan hated people of different races working together. They would never accept these people helping one another.

In 1929, in the eleventh grade, Rosa had to leave school to care for her sick grandmother. Three years later she married Raymond Parks, who was a barber. Raymond helped her go back to school. She graduated from her high school in 1934.

In l943, Rosa Parks began working for African-American rights. But Southerners who supported separation of the races had a set of rules to keep blacks from voting. These rules included things like special reading tests or a tax on all who wanted to vote. Rules like these were to prevent blacks from voting. So when Rosa went to vote, the white election officer said she could not. The next year, she tried to vote again. But still she was not allowed. Finally, in l945, she won her fight and voted.

In August 1955, she met Dr. Martin Luther King, Jr. He came to speak at a meeting of the civil rights group that she belonged to.

Then, on December 1 of that year, Rosa Parks refused to give up her bus seat to a white man. She spoke softly, but everyone heard her. She was arrested for breaking Jim Crow laws.

Her trial was on December 5, 1955. She was found guilty, fingerprinted, and sent to jail. Even though she was set free the same day, black people in her hometown were very angry. They felt she had been treated badly.

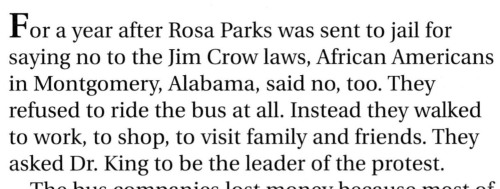

For a year after Rosa Parks was sent to jail for saying no to the Jim Crow laws, African Americans in Montgomery, Alabama, said no, too. They refused to ride the bus at all. Instead they walked to work, to shop, to visit family and friends. They asked Dr. King to be the leader of the protest.

The bus companies lost money because most of their riders were African Americans. The protest was a success.

Then, on December 21, 1956, African Americans were given the right to sit anywhere on public buses. At last they could stop walking. It was great to know that they had the power to change unfair laws. African Americans felt the new year would be different. They felt that life would be fairer.

The laws across the country started to change for the better. The new laws said blacks and whites had the same rights in public places. They could all eat at the same restaurants, ride the same buses, and go to the same schools. But some people hated these laws and fought the changes they brought.

Dr. King and other leaders of the civil rights movement wanted to make sure people obeyed the new laws. He and many others marched and worked to make the laws even better. In 1968, Dr. King was killed because he worked for these changes. But his work and his dream of freedom still live today.

Rosa Parks had lost her job because of the bus protest. She moved to Detroit. For a while she had to take in sewing to earn a living. But she did not stop working for everyone's equal rights.

In 1965, she began working for Congressman John Conyers who was a civil rights leader. In 1987 she founded the Rosa and Raymond Parks Institute for Self-Development, which helps young black people.

Rosa Parks still talks to people all over the country about civil rights. She also still works to help young people who have problems. She was mugged in 1994, but Ms. Parks says "...we should not let fear overwhelm us. We must remain strong. We must not give up hope; we can overcome."

## Key Dates

**1913**  Born in Tuskegee, Alabama, on February 4.

**1924**  Enters Miss Alice White's School in Montgomery, Alabama.

**1929**  Leaves school in the eleventh grade to care for her sick grandmother.

**1932**  Marries Raymond Parks, a barber.

**1943**  Becomes secretary of Montgomery branch of National Association for the Advancement of Colored People (NAACP).

**1955**  Meets Dr. Martin Luther King, Jr.
Refuses to give up her bus seat to white man and is arrested for breaking "Jim Crow" laws on December 1.
She is tried, found guilty, and jailed on December 5.

**1956**  Montgomery bus boycott runs all year.
City buses are legally integrated on December 21. African Americans win the right to sit anywhere.

**1979**  Wins the Spingarn Medal for her work in civil rights.

**1987**  Founds the Rosa and Raymond Parks Institute for Self-Development with Elaine Steele.

**1995**  Speaks to the Million-Man March in Washington, D.C. Introduced as the "Mother of the Civil Rights Movement."